S0-AGJ-919

LION

ELEPHANT

LEOPARD

BUFFALO

RHINOCEROS

THE BIG FIVE Once heralded by hunters as the five most dangerous and elusive animals; today, The Big Five are free to explore a vast African landscape. For their intriguing habits, noble stature and as representatives of this southerly continent, The Big Five are an inspiration to those who travel from the furthest corners of the earth in response to the call of the wild.

Lethal predator alongside mighty herbivore: in this great kingdom on the African plains, all existence is in synergy with the laws of nature. There are those that rule and those that must obey; some have the skill of the hunter while for others, survival depends on outsmarting the predator.

A pride of lion and a nomadic elephant herd

As African as a bushveld sunrise… a tribal song… a rhythmic drumbeat, The Big Five, once at the mercy of the hunter's greed, are now upheld for their priceless heritage, and conservationists rally to protect and perpetuate each species. It is this commitment to Africa's animal kingdom that has recalled many species, such as the rhinoceros, from the brink of extinction.

Left: Curious buffalo
Right: White rhino mother and calf
Opposite: Distinctive markings of the leopard

ELEPHANT *(Loxodonta africana)* The heavyweight of The Big Five, renowned as unpredictable and dangerous, yet with a sense of family loyalty few other species exhibit. Where once African elephant dwindled in number to just 120, today, over 10 000 of these mighty creatures grace the sundrenched bushveld, divided only by their allegiance to the weathered matriarch of each herd.

Sunset highlights the profile of a bull elephant

Closely bound through their breeding, elephant exist in large herds - a family of females and their offspring commanded by the largest cow, the matriarch. Males leave the herd in adolescence to roam free and sire the next generation - a well-synchronised perpetuation of the species.

Above: Elephant herd on the move
Opposite: Elephant mothers show great affection for their young

As a means of communication, the set of the trunk conveys the message: playful and trusting or angered and deadly. A frightened elephant will curl the tip of the trunk increasingly as the fear intensifies. A straight, level trunk is a serious threat; pointed to the sky, it's an announcement of mayhem.

With trunks intertwined, young elephant express mutual affection

Youngsters and adolescents often indulge in a friendly tussle or playful game of roly-poly. But when dominance needs to be established, elephant bulls engage in a war of sheer strength, pushing with mighty force until the weaker accepts defeat and, exposed to the tusks of a triumphant winner, turns to flee.

Opposite: Youngsters at play
Above left: Cooling off at the waterhole
Above right: Vigilant and wary

Opposite and right: A female elephant is innately protective of the young, often risking her own safety when a youngster is hurt or in danger, whether or not the calf is her own

70 years in the African bushveld; a lifetime of freedom. When an ageing elephant falls the herd clearly expresses their grief, covering the body with their trunks and carrying out ritual greetings in a display of unconditional love and respect.

An imposing silhouette, the biggest of The Big Five

LEOPARD *(Panthera Pardus)* A perfect array of distinctive rosettes and a focussed stare; intense determination and a regal pose identify the leopard, a graceful creature yet a finely-tuned and deadly predator. Shy, well-camouflaged, and more active at night, leopard are the most elusive of Africa's Big Five.

Leopard poised to target a kill

Patience is indeed the leopard's virtue. Many hours may be spent waiting in ambush or skillfully stalking unsuspecting prey. Using every ounce of strength, leopard often haul the kill into the branches of a tree, away from determined scavengers.

Left: A skilled hunter
Opposite: Exquisite markings on a wheat-coloured coat provide superb camourflage for the solitary leopard

Agile and quick, leopard are largely nocturnal hunters. They are also unfussy in their selection of prey: any creature from a beetle to an antelope double its own weight is suitable sustenance.

An eager cub learns hunting skills from a watchful mother

In a dense thicket or other suitable clandestine hiding place, leopard mothers bear their young in litters of between one and three. A protective mother, she will move her cubs periodically to eliminate the risk of their discovery, and will hunt within a smaller radius to be closeby in their early days.

Opposite: Playfulness teaches the lesson of agility and speed
Above: Unless well hidden, leopard cubs are vulnerable to larger predators

For young predators, the skills of the hunt must be learned before independent life is possible. Once they leave the sanctuary of the family unit, leopard live and hunt alone - solitary creatures drawn to their own kind only to perpetuate the species.

Left and opposite: Leopard escape the bushveld heat by climbing into the branches of a tree

Being essentially adaptable, leopard can tolerate varied habitats, from the searing heat of the desert to the relative cool of the forest - and have also been known to live close to human habitation, a lethal threat to livestock.

Opposite and above: Leopard against a woodland backdrop

WHITE RHINOCEROS *(Ceratotherium simum)* Relics of a bygone era, the rhinoceros represents a once widespread family of horned beasts that spanned 30 genera, including the largest land mammal yet recorded - a 5.5 metre giant.

White rhinoceros and calf splash through a waterhole

At over 2000 kilograms, the white rhinoceros is twice the weight of the black, rendered unmistakable by virtue of its larger head and well-defined square lip, suited to life as a grazer on the open plains.

Left: Bulky contours of a mature white rhino
Opposite: Mother and calf graze contentedly

Colossal in stature and big-hearted as a family unit, rhinoceros are usually found in small groups of mothers and offspring, while the bulls leave the confines of the family when they reach adolescence to discover territories of their own.

Opposite and above: Security lies in keeping together at all times

BLACK RHINOCEROS (*Diceros bicornis*)

Rhino horn, a weapon essential to the animal in territorial conflicts, is also a highly prized component of some traditional eastern medicines, and hunting caused a severe depletion in numbers. With modern day conservation efforts, the rhinoceros species - although still threatened - is no longer on the endangered list: a priceless heritage for generations to come.

A group of black rhinoceros in lush green surrounds

A hooked upper lip suitable for plucking leaves from woody trees, identifies the black rhinoceros - a short-tempered creature which, despite its bulk, is capable of a split-second change in direction and a fearsome charge certain to intimidate any intruder.

Opposite and right: Impressive proportions of the black rhinoceros

Seemingly placid and unperturbed, apparently encumbered and slow - yet their response to stimuli may be quick beyond belief, and deadly beyond comparison.   When disturbed, black rhino flee with calves in pursuit: the white rhinoceros tends to leave the scene with the calf taking the lead.

Weathered, wary and watchful black rhino

LION *(Panthera Leo)*   Unrivalled leader of the animal kingdom, born to a life of supremacy.   Africa's largest carnivores are renowned as much for their ruthless hunting tactics and impressive show of might, as they are for the stability of their family sanctuaries.

Left: *Regal profile of a young lion*
Opposite: *Male and female* ^{mir-}
rored at a tranquil waterhole

A typical pride may consist of only two adult males, several related females, and their cubs of assorted ages. Cubs are often killed by adult males in an endeavour to sire their own offspring. Cubs remain with the pride until territorial males force younger males to migrate when they reach three years of age.

Opposite and right: Whether playful or in anger, a well-timed snarl warns when tolerance is reaching a limit

A lioness conceals her cubs while she hunts. The pride is a co-operative unit where responsibility for protecting the young and shepherding those that stray is a shared concern: one adult lioness eagerly babysits while the youngsters' mothers go hunting.

Family bonds unite the pride

Play is more than exercise: it is a learning experience. A young cub will blunder toward another, equally uncoordinated sibling, missing it hopelessly. Yet with regular practice at play-time, the young hunter soon learns to strike its victim with a fair degree of accuracy.

Opposite and above: The pride at play

The female lion assumes responsibility for providing sustenance for the pride: she is the hunter. Yet when a kill is made it is the male who eats first, followed by females and juveniles. Cubs learn the hierarchy of the pride by waiting until last, often going hungry. Only half the cubs born actually survive to maturity.

Left: Mother and cubs at the waterhole
Opposite: Adults are tolerant of cubs - but there are limits

BUFFALO *(Syncerus Caffer)* A giant herbivore with a short temper - and a sturdy set of horns to put to good use in defence against any perceived threat. Buffalo are gregarious creatures found in large herds, chiefly for protection against that ruthless predator, the lion.

Opposite and right: Buffalo are kept free of ticks and parasites by the eager red billed ox-pecker

Non-territorial roamers, buffalo adhere to a distinct hierarchy of dominant bulls and clans of related cows, with a "navigator" appointed to lead the herd to pastures and water.

Left and opposite: Buffalo are nomadic, settling only long enough to enjoy the grazing

A phenomenon unique to the wild kingdom is that of synchronised births. Mating generally takes place on a regular schedule, ensuring the young are born within a short period. Nature thus guarantees that the herds lose fewer young to predators than they would if births were sporadic: there is indeed safety in numbers.

Opposite: Roaming buffalo in search of good grazing
Above: African sunset

PHOTOGRAPHERS   D Allen - *pages 19, 48, 56, back cover*
P Chadwick - *page 7, 27, 28* M Craig-Cooper - *page 1* R de la Harpe
- *pages cover, 3a, 10, 39, 43, 51* N Dennis - *page 3b, 8, 12, 15a, 16, 36,
44, 46, 52-54, 61* R du Toit - *page 2c, 23, 31, 59, 62, 63* M Harvey
- *pages 2a, 4, 6b, 11, 15b, 17, 26, 35, 37, 47, 64* J Keywood - *page 20-22,
49* G Lopez-Espina / Essentia Images - *pages 14, 25, 55* P Macfarlane
- *page 2b, 41, 60* M Reardon - *page 40* H van der berg - *page 32* J
Wakelin - *page 29, 30* S Vincent - *page 58* Unknown - *page 34*

Produced by Art Publishers (Pty) Ltd

Durban, Johannesburg, Cape Town

*All rights reserved. No part of this publication may be reproduced in any form
without the prior written consent of the publisher*

The Big Five: one of Africa's many natural wonders